WE WERE HERE FIRST
THE NATIVE AMERICANS

THE
ZUNI

Tamra B. Orr

PURPLE TOAD
PUBLISHING

WE WERE HERE FIRST
THE NATIVE AMERICANS

The Apache of the Southwest
The Blackfeet
The Cherokee
The Cheyenne
The Choctaw
The Comanche
The Creek
The Inuit of the Arctic
The Iroquois of the Northeast
The Lenape
The Navajo
The Nez Perce of the Pacific Northwest
The Seminole
The Sioux of the Great Northern Plains
The Zuni

Printing   1   2   3   4   5   6   7   8   9

Publisher's Cataloging-in-Publication Data
Orr, Tamra B.
  Zuni / written by Tamra B. Orr.
    p. cm.
Includes bibliographic references, glossary, and
index.
  ISBN 9781624692918
1. Zuni Indians--Juvenile literature. 2. Indians of
North America--New Mexico--Juvenile literature. I.
Series: We Were Here First: The Native Americans.
  E99.Z9 2017
  978.9004
Library of Congress Control Number: 2016957224

eBook ISBN: 9781624692925

CONTENTS

Zuni homes were built into the landscape. They had flat roofs and multiple levels connected by ladders.

CHAPTER 1
A NEW ARRIVAL

Slowly, the sky began to lighten. The rustle of night animals faded away, while the birds ruffled their feathers and began their morning songs. The first rays of sunlight crept over the horizon, announcing the return of Sun Father and the start of a new day.

Inside Luna's house, her newborn baby brother woke. He pushed his feet and hands out against the warm sand bed next to Luna's mother. Without making a sound, Grandmother Taci knelt down next to the baby. Luna held her breath. She had been waiting for this moment for eight whole days.

Luna's paternal grandmother had arrived when the baby was born. She made a bed for the little one and gave him a gentle bath. She also came to pray to the Raw People to protect the baby and keep him safe and strong.

The eight days had felt terribly long to Luna. She wanted to be outside playing with her friends, but she also wanted to stay inside with her mother, grandmother, and baby brother. All day long, she would run outside, scamper down the ladder, and join her friends. Then, moments later, she would climb back up the ladder to check on everyone.

"Luna!" her grandmother had scolded her. "In or out!"

But today, finally, Luna's new brother could come outside. In the dawn's light, Grandmother Taci carefully washed her new grandchild's head. Then she dusted cornmeal over the baby's hands to honor the sacred plant. Finally, she picked up the little one and stepped outside. The sun was just rising in the eastern sky. Grandmother turned her face to the sunshine and began reciting the prayer Luna had been waiting to hear:

> *Now this is the day.*
> *Our child,*
> *Into the daylight*
> *You will go out standing. . . .*
> *Now this day*
> *Our father, Dawn priests,*
> *Have come out standing to their sacred place, . . .*
> *Our child, it is your day. . . .*
> *The flesh of the white corn, prayer meal,*
> *To our sun father*
> *This prayer meal we offer.*
> *May your road be fulfilled.*
> *Reaching to the road of your sun father, . . .*
> *In your thoughts may we live.*[1]

As Grandmother finished the special prayer, she glanced over and saw her granddaughter quietly standing behind her and smiled.

"Good morning, little Luna," she said. "Did you come to greet Sun Father with me?"

Luna nodded. "Do you have a name for him yet?" she asked, pointing to the baby. Not knowing what to call her brother was hard. She was eager to know what name her grandmother would choose for him.

"Not yet," Grandmother Taci said with a shake of her head. "We must wait until we know if he is as strong and healthy as you were when you were born. We will have to see if he can walk the road that Sun Father has chosen

6

Pueblo homes were quite simple inside. Family members from several generations tended to sit on the floor while they cooked, made tools for the home, and talked.

for him. Evil spirits are always watching for little souls, and that is why I pray to the Raw People to keep your brother safe. Once we know that, then I will select just the right name for him."

Luna nodded solemnly. She knew the rules. "But Grandma," she whispered, "I think Halian would be the perfect name for such a lovely boy."

Grandmother Taci smiled. Halian had been the name of her husband, a man she still missed years after he had taken the journey to the Village of Souls. He had lived a long and honorable life. "I think that is a splendid name too," she agreed. Luna jumped up and down quietly. "But time will tell," Grandmother added.

Luna looked down at the ground. She prayed to Sun Father and the Raw People that they would keep her baby brother safe.

The sun's arrival each morning reminded the Zuni to be thankful and stay on the path in life that Sun Father had determined for each of them.

As the sun pushed away the last of the night's darkness, Luna, Grandmother Taci, and the baby all went back into the quiet house. Luna wanted to sleep just a few minutes longer. As she closed her eyes, she smiled once more. Her little brother would make such a grand Halian.

The Two Spirits: We-Wha

In a number of Native American tribes, some men dressed and lived as women, and some women dressed and lived as men. The term for this lifestyle was *berdache*. Berdache people were accepted by the tribe and were considered a third gender. They were also believed to be exceptional in some way.

One famous Zuni who lived this way was We-Wha, a boy born in 1849. Like other young men, We-Wha was trained in battle skills, hunting, weaving, and becoming a kachina. Unlike other boys, he also learned how to cook, gather firewood, and make pottery. Because he was considered both male and female, We-Wha was also known as "Two Spirits."

We-Wha was so talented at weaving and making pottery that he was asked to make clothing and pots for museums across the country. He was one of the first Native Americans to sell tribal art to non-Indians.

In 1886, We-Wha went to Washington, D.C., to meet President Grover Cleveland. As an ambassador of the Zuni tribe, he was introduced

We-Wha

as a Zuni princess. He demonstrated his weaving skills and charmed everyone he met. No one in Washington realized he was male.[2]

The Zuni built huge villages. Their hundreds of rooms could house more than 1,000 people. This village was built on top of the mountain El Morro.

CHAPTER 2
THE A'SHIWI

Like many early Native Americans, Zuni ancestors were nomads. Plant growth and animal groups changed with the seasons, so the Zuni moved from place to place as the seasons changed. They lived in small camps and spent their days in search of food. Men hunted, and women looked for wild plants, nuts, and berries. It was a busy life, and starvation was a constant threat.

Much of that fear and lifestyle changed around 700 to 800 CE. The Zuni people began to build permanent villages along the Zuni River in the Southwest (see map, page 40). They called themselves A'Shiwi, or "the flesh people."

Their first village was Halona. From there, the tribe spread out and created six other communities. They settled in the valleys and on top of mesas. All the villages were within a 25-mile radius, and they became known as the Seven Cities of Cibola (see-BOH-lah, or SEE-buh-luh). One of the biggest communities was on top of El Morro, a mountain in western New Mexico. Even though the Zuni were largely peaceful people, they used these high villages to keep an eye on the land in all directions.

Hunting deer and elk was a regular part of Zuni life. The forests were full of different animals, and hunting them kept the tribe from starving.

Life in these six villages was much different than the nomadic lifestyle. Because the land featured plains, deserts, forests, and mountains, game was plentiful. There was no need to keep moving to find it. The men could hunt a variety of animals, from the larger elk, deer, bear, and antelope to the smaller rabbits, mice, foxes, and even reptiles. Women learned to use shrubs, cacti, and other plants for cooking. It was a good life, but it was about to change.

Spanish Invaders

By the 1500s, the Zuni had learned a great many things. For years they had been trading with other tribes throughout New Mexico and California. Along with trading items, they also traded ideas. The Zuni learned how to plant crops such as maize, or corn. Since they lived in a hot, dry area, they also learned how to move water from the Zuni River to their fields. This type of irrigation allowed them to grow corn, squash, beans, tobacco, and sunflowers. They traded these items, in addition to turquoise, jewelry, and pottery, for exotic items such as parrot feathers, seashells, copper, and coral.[1]

In 1539, a friar or priest named Marcos de Niza was exploring the Southwest. He told people in Spain that he had personally seen the famous Seven Cities of Cibola. According to legend, the cities were paved with gold. He had only seen it from afar, but he said, "It appears to be a very beautiful city, the best that I have seen in these parts."[2] This was very exciting news to Spanish explorers.

Seen from afar, the city of El Dorado seemed to glow with light from countless amounts of gold.

When Coronado arrived in Zuni land, he was surprised and frustrated to find thousands of people but no gold.

More than 300 Spanish soldiers, and 1,000 Native American slaves, followed Francisco Vasquez de Coronado to the Zuni area to see what was there.[3] They were beyond disappointed. Instead of roads paved with gold and other wild treasures, they simply saw Zuni villages. Had the priest lied? No one is sure. Some believe he saw mesas bathed in sunlight, which gave them a golden glow. Others say he just made the story up to get attention and fame.

The Spanish explorers were terribly unhappy. They had spent huge amounts of money in their quest. Now, they would have nothing to show for it.

The Spaniards stayed in the Zuni village for three months, and then pushed on. They traveled hundreds more miles in search of the city of gold—but found nothing like it. Instead of returning home, Coronado set up a new Spanish colony on the Rio Grande in New Mexico.

The Spanish invasion changed the Zuni way of life. It introduced the idea that people from other parts of the world might want to take control and make demands. The foreigners also brought sicknesses that killed many Native Americans.

On the other hand, the Spanish introduced new crops to the Zuni, including wheat and peaches. They also brought sheep and horses to the region.

Taking Back Control

Once the Spanish had settled into the area, it was not long before more explorers came. By 1632, several Catholic missions had been established in Zuni villages. Native Americans who did not accept the new religion were often punished. Some were even killed.

As the years passed, the Zuni and other tribes in the area grew angry and resentful of the Spanish. Finally, in 1680, the Pueblo Revolt began. Native Americans killed area priests, burned down churches, and sent Spanish settlers running. For their protection, the Zuni left their villages and moved into a settlement on top of Dowa Yalanne, or Corn Mountain. They remained on this sacred mountain for 12 years, until the Spanish returned once more.[4]

The flat top of Dowa Yalanne made it the perfect place to settle while the Zuni outwaited the Spanish.

In 1692, the Spanish came back to Zuni territory. This time they were lead by Diego de Varga, a Spanish general. He came peacefully, apologizing for the earlier mistreatments.

The Zuni came down from Corn Mountain, but they did not return to their different communities. Instead, they all went to live in their first village, Halona.

Although the Zuni were not an aggressive tribe, they were often attacked by the Apache and Navajo. In 1705, the Zuni signed an agreement with the Spanish. The foreigners could stay in the area if, in return, they would help protect the Zuni from further attacks. The Zuni remained under Spanish control for decades. When Mexico gained independence from Spain in 1821, Zuni territory became part of the Republic of Mexico.

When the United States went to war with Mexico, the fate of Zuni land was in limbo again. In 1848, the Treaty of Guadalupe Hidalgo was signed. It made New Mexico part of the United States.

In 1877, President Rutherford B. Hayes signed an executive order that created the Zuni Reservation. The order recognized the Zuni government and promised their land would not be taken. The area allotted to the tribe was about one-tenth the size of their territory before the Spanish explorers

came. More land was added to their reservation several times throughout the years. By 1940, it had expanded to more than 400,000 acres.

The Zuni have continued to fight in court for the return of more of their land. In 1984, they won back a sacred piece of land known as *Koluwala-wa*.[5]

One of the things that make the Zuni unique among Native American tribes is that they were never forced to leave their original homelands. The territory they originally settled is where they stayed. In fact, the Zuni still live there today.

President Rutherford B. Hayes

"The Mockingbird" and the Zuni Language

Curtis Cook (right) wanted to make sure that the rich heritage of the Zuni people was captured in print.

In the 1960s, Curtis Cook, a linguist, wanted to help create a version of the Bible for the Zuni people. He discovered, however, that their language had never been put into written form. Capturing the language before it disappeared became Cook's mission. "I became concerned that many of their old stories and the richness of their history would be lost to posterity as the elders, who were the storytellers, began to die off," he told *Deseret News*.

For 15 years, Cook lived with the Zuni people. Seven Native American elders, each over 100 years old, told him their stories. Cook made more than 300 voice recordings and written documents of the Zuni's myths, traditions, and tales. He constantly repeated all he heard, earning him the Zuni nicknames of "The Mockingbird" and "The Locust."

Cook's tapes, notes, and papers were put into boxes and stored for decades. Then, in 2006, the Library of Congress asked Cook to share those documents. Researchers there wanted to make sure the Zuni language was preserved. They also wanted to share it with the rest of the world.

Because of Cook's work, Zuni children can still learn to read and write their native language. Cook is pleased that his years of hard work have finally been helpful. "When people get their language in writing, it launches a whole new era," he told *Deseret News*. "We take notes so we can remember."[6]

The underground kiva was a holy and mysterious place for the Zuni.

CHAPTER 3
CLIFF HOMES, CRAFTS, AND CROPS

The Zuni built sturdy homes called pueblos. These homes were made with local materials: stones, clay, and straw. The stones were fit close together and then glued into place with adobe, a mixture of clay and straw. Adobe dries hard under the sun's hot rays.

Adobe is not what made the Zuni homes so unusual, though. These homes were built under the overhang of cliffs or along sheer canyon walls. They were stacked up like today's apartment buildings. One family's flat roof was another one's floor. Each unit was home to a single family. Rooms on either side of it were for relatives, such as grandparents, aunts, and uncles. The apartments were all connected not by stairways, but by long wooden ladders. The ladders were pulled up at night so that no one could stop by for an unexpected visit.

In addition to these adobe homes, each village had at least one kiva. These sacred buildings were often built underground. Some were square, while others were circular. They had no doors or windows. People could get in and out only by a hole in the roof. Kivas were used for spiritual ceremonies and secret rites. Often they had benches around the walls and a fireplace in the middle.[1] All men in the village became part of a kiva from a very early age.

Zuni Women

In the Zuni tribe, the mother was the head of the household. The family name was shared through her. After marriage, daughters stayed in the same household in which they were born, but sons went to live with their new wife's family. Women traditionally wore knee-length cotton dresses known as *mantas*. They fastened at the shoulder, similar to a toga. After missionaries came to the region, women began wearing light shirts under their mantas.

Food was the center of women's work. It was their job to prepare it, cook it, and preserve it. Corn was the center of the Zuni diet, and it was roasted, boiled, or crushed. It was used in stews, bread, and cakes. It was turned into popcorn or eaten on the cob. Women spent a great deal of time grinding corn. They also ground nuts and seeds to be added to various dishes.

Women ground corn every day. It was a time-consuming and tiring chore.

In addition to cooking the food, Zuni women dedicated time to growing it. They had small gardens, with each plant in its own small square with mud walls. These walls helped keep water in and wind, animals, dogs, and children out. This pattern of squares earned the gardens the name of waffle gardens. Women had to keep each plant watered—not an easy chore in the hot, dry climate of New Mexico! The Zuni would fill large jars called *ollas* with water from the nearby Zuni River or wells. Then, they would put the jars on top of their head and walk back to the garden,

Zuni women had amazing balance. They could walk long distances with heavy water jars on their heads.

where they would use gourd dippers to water each plant individually. Women grew plants, but they also searched for wild plants nearby. Some of these plants were used for medicine, while others—such as watercress, wild peas, and parsnips—were added to the daily diet.[2]

Zuni Men

While women were busy with the home, food, and children, men focused on making tools for hunting, such as bows and arrows. They also made gardening tools such as shovels, hoes, and rakes. They tended the livestock: sheep, goats, and even wild turkeys were farmed. Sheep and goats were used for their wool and meat. Men often had to make sure that their livestock did not wander into a nearby farmer's field and do damage. To prevent this, they would haul in brush, broken limbs, and other natural materials to block off pathways the animals might try to take.[3]

Zuni men typically wore breechcloths or short kilts. Many also wore cloth headbands. The men in the Zuni village acted as priests, political leaders, and warriors. On the other hand, both men and women could take on the roles of storytellers, musicians, artists, and healers. Women specialized in making decorative pottery, while men typically made baskets and used looms to weave clothing. Both wore deerskin moccasins, and men and women wore their hair long in a figure eight. This hairstyle was known as *chongo*. Silver and turquoise jewelry frequently decorated their thick, black hair.

Some Zuni were medicine men. They were experts in understanding and using wild plants.

Although baskets were practical, they were also very beautiful and required a great deal of skill to make.

Zuni Craftsmanship

When the Zuni first made their crafts, a number of them were for practical use. Baskets were used for carrying or storing food. Rugs were used on floors and as seats and beds. All of these were woven from plant fibers and branches from trees such as the willow. Pottery was for cooking and serving meals. Tools were used to garden and hunt.

Other items, however, were used for spiritual reasons. A special type of carving, known as a fetish, was a symbol of the animal spirits. Fetishes were hand carved from a variety of materials and then blessed by a tribal priest. Native Americans believed that these carvings could offer protection, luck, or healing. They were typically carved in the shapes of bears, wolves, eagles, or badgers. Some Zuni used whatever stones they could find. Others used turquoise or alabaster.[4]

This eagle fetish has been carefully carved to show the bird's feathers and bright eyes.

Fetishes were also used like a tool in order to improve a particular skill. Robin Dunlap, a Zuni who has helped organize Zuni art shows, explained this in an article in the *Sante Fe New Mexican*. "What they were doing was carrying an animal that did the thing well that they wanted to do well. It's like a tool," she added. "If you are going deer hunting, what animal is going to be the best hunter of the deer? The cougar. So to this day they carry a mountain lion with them, and when they honor the mountain lion's ability to hunt the deer, they're remembering to focus on their ability to hunt the deer. Because what they say is, if Great Spirit made mountain lion and Great Spirit made me, we're connected, and it's just about honoring that connection."[5]

Other Zuni took up the skill of silversmithing, or making jewelry. In 1872, a Zuni man named Lanyade learned from a Navajo how to make silver jewelry. In turn, Lanyade taught others.[6] In the beginning, men were the artists. Later, women also learned the skill. Some artists focused on using small bits of turquoise to create patterns. Others combined turquoise with pieces of coral and seashells to create an image.[7]

Today, Zuni pottery, carvings, and jewelry are still highly prized. Current artists produce pieces for museums, collectors of fine art, and others who love and appreciate beauty.

Lanyade the Silversmith

The Soyal Solstice Ceremony

Honoring and respecting the sun reflects one of the most basic beliefs of the Zuni people.

To the Zuni, as well as many other tribes, the sun means life. It gives warmth and light and helps grow crops. To show their respect for the sun, the Zuni held the Soyal Solstice Ceremony. It was also known as the Great Feast of the Winter Solstice. The event was always held on December 21, as that was the shortest day of year—it had the fewest hours of sunshine. The ceremony was done to remind the sun to come back after it had traveled so far away, and thus, to bring back summertime.[8]

The kachina would dance, shake prayer sticks, pray, beat drums, and make offerings. Dancers wore masks. They decorated their clothes with shells, antlers, fur, or leather. This dance is still performed in New Mexico. People from all over the world come to watch the kachina call back the sun.

The Zuni, like other Native American tribes, believed in the use of prayer sticks to appeal to the Raw People for protection. Here, a Zuni man places a prayer stick beside a pool of water.

CHAPTER 4
RELIGION AND THE RAW PEOPLE

For the Zuni people, religion was the center of the world. Prayers were said daily, and spirits were found in everything from plants and animals to clouds, rocks, baskets, and carvings. A peaceful tribe, the Zuni looked for balance and harmony in everything they did.

Some of the most important gods in the Zuni world were Sun Father, Moon Mother, and Earth Mother. These gods made sure the sun rose and set every day, and made rain fall from the sky. The Zuni loved and respected these gods. They often sang and danced to drums to honor the deities.

When the Zuni prayed for healthy children, good hunts, strong crops, or long, happy lives, they were often praying to a group of spirits and gods known as the Raw People. The Raw People were divine beings who looked out for the people. In return, some of the tribal members were called Daylight People. Their job was to honor the deities by offering food, such as raw fruits and vegetables, cornmeal, or tobacco smoke. Prayers to the Raw People often involved the use of prayer sticks.[1]

The Zuni made many of their prayer sticks from the wood of willow trees. They would often carve a face into the stick,

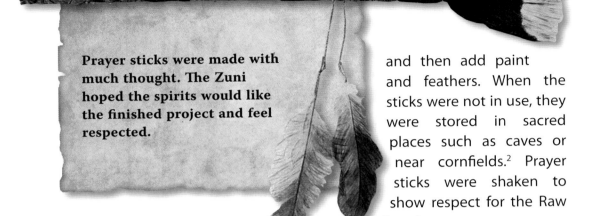

Prayer sticks were made with much thought. The Zuni hoped the spirits would like the finished project and feel respected.

and then add paint and feathers. When the sticks were not in use, they were stored in sacred places such as caves or near cornfields.[2] Prayer sticks were shaken to show respect for the Raw People.

The Kachinas

For the Zuni tribe, a kachina was many things. To the elders, he was a spirit, a father figure, and a masked dancer. To children, he was like a bogeyman, a creature that might come to the house at night to punish naughty behavior. Kachinas were actually male tribal members who put on bright, colorful masks and costumes. They were then believed to have supernatural or magical powers. The people prayed to them for more rain or more children, healthy crops, or healthy lives. The kachina danced at special occasions, such as the winter or summer solstice and the autumn harvest.

Kachina dancers

Kachina dolls reflected how seriously the Zuni felt about their gods and spirits. The dolls took time and talent to create, and they were treated with respect.

These dances sometimes lasted for hours. They were so difficult and complex that it took days and days of practice for the dancers to learn all the steps.

The Zuni also made kachina dolls. These dolls were typically made from the roots of trees. The wood was smoothed and shaped using hammers, knives, and hatchets. Small pieces were carved to make accessories for the dolls. They might have rattles, bows and arrows, or headdresses. Next, the dolls were carefully painted, using natural dyes and brushes made from yucca plants.[3] Sometimes beads or stones were added as earrings, necklaces, or other jewelry. Animal hides and fur were used to clothe the dolls, along with bird feathers. Finally, the mask was added. While these dolls were given to children, they were not considered toys. Instead, they were a way to learn more about and honor the gods all around them.

When Death Arrived

When a Zuni tribe member died, it was time to prepare the body for burial—and the soul to go to the afterworld. The paternal aunt in the family was usually called on to bathe the body, rub it in cornmeal, and dress it in new clothes. After the body was dressed, each piece of the new clothing was cut. The holes allowed the spirits that lived in the clothing to escape and travel to the afterworld with the person's soul.[4]

When someone dies, the entire family gathers to cry and mourn. While brothers are often assigned the task of digging the grave, others gather the deceased's possessions to place in the grave with the body. The person's spouse often mourns for days. Those days are long—the spouse cannot have a fire or eat meat. He or she must use only cold water and stay quiet and alone.[5] During those four days, the deceased person's soul travels to a village of souls below the Sacred Lake, about 65 miles southwest of Zuni.[6] There they will be with friends and family who have died before.

People gather to say a final goodbye at a funeral in Pueblo of Isleta, New Mexico, in 1898.

The Zuni have honored their religious beliefs for centuries—and it has not always been easy. Over the years, missionaries from a variety of faiths tried to convince the Native Americans that their beliefs were wrong. When the Catholic missionaries forbade the people to say their own prayers, the people sang their prayers in cornfields and claimed they were planting songs.[7]

Modern Zuni practice many of the same religious dances and rituals. They sprinkle cornmeal at sunrise, and at least one man in each family devotes his life to religion.

The beliefs of the Zuni and the faith of the Spanish Catholic missionaries were very different.

Edward Wemytewa, a former tribal councilman in Zuni, stated in *The Smithsonian*, "There's one key to understanding Zuni. And it's that the dances that take place here in the plaza are the heart of who we are. All the movement and colors, the singing and the sounds of the bells and the drums echoing off the walls—all this touches your spirit. From the day you are born as a Zuni until the day you leave this world, this is within you."[8]

Missionaries who tried to covert Zuni children to Christianity often had a hard time learning the complex Native American language.

The Zuni Language

One way the Zuni preserve their rich history is through their language. The Zuni language is considered unlike any other Indian tongue. It includes many breaths and pauses, and each one has a specific meaning. Over thousands of years, it has changed very little, but there is a growing fear that the language will eventually fade away.

A study in 2000 showed that 73 percent of the Zuni people were using their native language in the home.[9] Edison Vicenti is a former computer engineer who became a kachina priest. He told *The Smithsonian*, "If we lose our language, we lose the base of our religion and culture. And if we lose our religion, we lose what binds us together as Zuni. It is like the roots of a tree; if the tree is uprooted or the roots contaminated, then it dies. It is the same with us. And we can't let that happen."[10]

Kiva Initiation

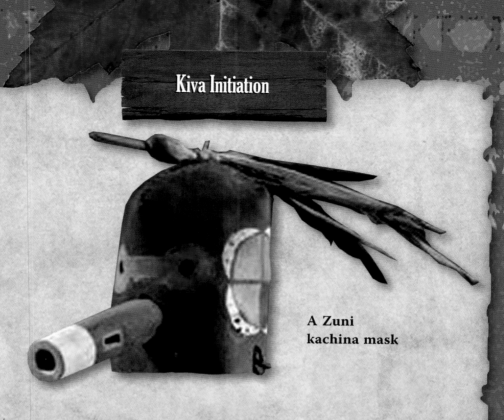

A Zuni kachina mask

Male Zuni tribal members belonged to one of six kachinas. The initiation rites into the kachina were often a bit scary, but they were an accepted part of the culture. When a boy reached the age of five or six, his godfather, or a non-related male sworn to watch over the child's training, came to the child's home. The godfather's wife washed the young boy, and then the godfather carried the child into the kiva. There the tribe's adult men were dressed in kachina clothes and masks. The boys were gathered together and gently whipped (not to cause pain). Even though the children knew the kachinas were gods, there to protect and take care of them, this was still a somewhat frightening experience.

Years would go by until the second stage of the initiation began. When the boys were between ten and twelve years old, they returned to the kiva. This time they were whipped harder. When they were done, the men took off their masks and revealed that they were, indeed, human beings, and not gods. Then the men handed the boys the whips and masks and switched roles.[11]

Zuni crafts are often sold at bazaars, craft shows, and other events.

CHAPTER 5
TODAY'S
ZUNI

On a steamy August afternoon in Santa Fe, New Mexico, a large group of talented artists filled the Scottish Rite Temple. Each artist was a Zuni tribal member. Their handcrafted pottery, jewelry, and paintings were on display—and for sale. They also brought different types of fetishes, carved from rocks, shells, and antlers. The event was organized to showcase the beauty of Zuni art. Many believe the show was one of the largest gatherings of Zuni artists ever held.

The Zuni Show featured more than just vendors with their art. It also had a number of dancers. Young women danced with pots carefully balanced on their head. Other artists performed traditional dances in the center's courtyard. It was an exciting opportunity for today's Native Americans to display their unique and lovely art and history to the rest of the world.[1]

Virtually all Zuni people live in Zuni, New Mexico. While their lives have become much more modern over the years, they have also preserved many of their tribe's traditions and rituals. Some are farmers, raising corn, beans, squash, and other vegetables. Others continue to raise livestock, especially sheep.[2] The majority of people, however, focus on the arts their ancestors learned so long ago. They make beautiful rugs, clothing, and baskets. They use special tools to carve fetishes. They combine coral, shells, turquoise, and silver to make jewelry. As they state on one of their web sites, "With perhaps 80 percent of our workforce involved in making arts, we are indeed an 'artist colony.' "[3]

Tourism is also part of the Zuni's economy. The Native Americans welcome visitors to their pueblo, which covers about 700 square miles and is home to more than 10,000 people. Visitors are reminded that although they are allowed to watch the tribe's religious activities, such as dances, there are some rules to follow. "We ask that visitors respect our cultural privacy by following the appropriate [manners] and guidelines," they state on the tourism site. "Our ceremonial activities are what make the Zuni people unique."[4]

Visitors from all over the world come to watch Pueblo dancers display their traditional costumes, rituals, and dances.

Native American tribes, including the Zuni, still band together to protect lands that are sacred or historically important to them.

Sacred Sites

The Zuni continue to fight for and protect their land. In 2003, for example, the tribe successfully protested against the Salt River Project. This private utility company wanted to mine land near the sacred Zuni Salt Lake. The following year, a similar battle took place. When a company wanted to mine the sacred Woodruff Butte, Zuni, Navajo, and Hopis worked together to save it. The U.S. Court of Appeals ruled on the side of the Native Americans. The land would be protected.

The Zuni have worked hard to ensure that other sacred sites and artifacts are protected by law. They also care deeply about area wildlife. For example, in 1999, they opened an eagle aviary. It takes care of injured and sick bald and golden eagles. These large birds have always meant a great deal to the tribe. "We Zuni have always considered them members of the family," Steve Boone, the pueblo's lieutenant governor, said about the eagles. "We raised them from fledglings, and they lived among us their entire lifespan. We took care of them, and they took care of us."[5] In addition to caring for the birds, the Zuni also collect the feathers the birds drop for use in religious ceremonies.

Each year, at the beginning of September, the tribe members of Zuni, New Mexico, host the Zuni Tribal Fair. They have been doing so for more than 50 years. The event is a way to share their traditions and history with the rest of the world. In addition to dances, parades, concerts, and exhibits, the fair features three beauty pageants, each one designed for a different age group.[6]

By maintaining their traditions and honoring the past, the Zuni have made it possible to connect modern living with time-honored rituals and beliefs. It is a lifestyle that even Sun Father may appreciate.

A rich past added to a strong present will almost certainly make for a brighter future for the Zuni.

The Sha'lak'o Festival

Sha'lak'o dancers

In late December, at the winter solstice, the Zuni say goodbye to the old year and welcome the new one. A dozen costumed figures dance their way through the villages. These dancers are the Sha'lak'o, or messengers of the gods. Their faces are covered by bird-like masks. Their costumes are made of painted buckskin and willow-wood frames. With their costumes, they are almost ten feet tall.

At the Sha'lak'o dance in 2011, a young Zuni boy walked into the center of town pretending to be the Fire God. He held a burning cedar torch in one hand, and balanced a bag of seeds over his shoulder with the other. His body was covered with circles of red, yellow, blue, and white. After him came the Rain God of the North, wearing a mask of black-and-white stripes, and a suit of white buckskin. He held a long, curved horn and wore sparkly jewelry.

Each year, the dancers keep dancing for several days. Just before the festival ends, the next year's dancers are chosen.[8]

Location: Pueblo of Zuni, New Mexico

Region: Southwest

States: New Mexico, Arizona

Land area: 408,404 acres

Traditional name: A'Shiwi ("The Flesh")

Current population:

10,228 (2010)

Hunted with blowguns

Lived in cliff dwellings

Never had to leave

homelands

Before 700 CE	Zuni ancestors live as nomads.
700 to 800 CE	The Zuni begin to build permanent villages along the Zuni River.
1500s	The Zuni have set up trade with other tribes throughout Mexico and California.
1539	Marcos de Niza reports to Spain that he has seen the Seven Cities of Cibola. His stories make people believe the legend that their streets are paved with gold.
1540	Francisco Vasquez de Coronado brings soldiers and slaves to Cibola.
1632	Catholic missionaries are living among the Zuni.
1680	The Pueblo Revolt begins. The Zuni move to Corn Mountain (Dowa Yalanne).
1692	Diego de Varga, a Spanish general, leads another expedition to Zuni territory.
1705	The Zuni sign an agreement with the Spanish, trading land for protection from neighboring tribes.
1821	Mexico gains independence from Spain. The Zuni are now under control of Mexico.
1848	The Treaty of Guadalupe Hidalgo is signed. Zuni territory, which is in New Mexico, becomes part of the United States.
1872	Zuni member Lanyade begins making silver jewelry.
1877	President Rutherford B. Hayes signs an order that creates the Zuni Reservation.
1881	The Southern Pacific Railroad brings more settlers and missionaries to New Mexico.
1940	The Zuni Reservation covers more than 400,000 acres.
1960	Curtis Cook begins recording the Zuni language.
1984	The Zuni win back the sacred piece of land known as Koluwala-wa.
2003	The tribe successfully protests against the Salt River Project, which would have destroyed their sacred Salt Lake.
2004	The Zuni help the Hopi save the sacred Woodruff Butte in Arizona from a mining company.
2016	A group of eight Zuni youth spend a month upgrading the walking trail at Chimney Rock National Monument in the San Juan National Forest. Their work is part of the Southwest Conservation Corps Ancestral Lands Program.

Chapter 1

1. Astrov, Margot. *The Winged Serpent: American Indian Prose and Poetry* (Boston: Beacon Press, 1992), p. 231.
2. "We-Wha." PBS.org.

Chapter 2

1. "Zuni—Economy," *Countries and Their Cultures*.
2. Drye, Willie. "Seven Cities of Cibola Legend Lures Conquistadors." *National Geographic*.
3. "AD 1540: The Zuni Resist a Conquistador but Retreat from Spanish Guns." *Native Voices*. U.S. National Library of Medicine.
4. Bonvillain, Nancy. *The Zuni* (New York: Chelsea House, 2011), pp. 138–139.
5. "Native American Legends: The Zuni: A Mysterious People." Legends of America.
6. Romero, Christine. "Arizona Man Helps Preserve Zuni Language." *Deseret News*. August 27, 2006.

Chapter 3

1. "Zuni Tribe." *War Paths to Peace Pipes*.
2. Bonvillain, Nancy. *The Zuni* (New York: Chelsea House, 2011), pp. 43–45.
3. Coburn, Kelly M., Edward Landa, Gail Wagner. "Of Silt and Ancient Voices: Water and the Zuni Land and People." National Center for Case Study Teaching in Science.
4. Widner, Ellis. "Fetish Carvers Show How It's Done." Philly.com, March 4, 1994.
5. Weiderman, Paul. "Hearts Beating in the Rock: The Zuni Show." *Santa Fe New Mexican*, August 19, 2016.
6. "History of American Indian Jewelry Making." *American Indian Originals*.
7. Bonvillain, p. 105.

8. "Soyal Solstice Ceremony.' *War Paths to Peace Pipes*.

Chapter 4

1. "Zuni." *World History*, September 4, 2015.
2. "Prayer Stick," *War Paths to Peace Pipes*.
3. Padgett, Ken. "Guide to Hopi Kachina Dolls." Kachina.us.2005.
4. Ibid., p. 30.
5. Ibid.
6. Parsons, Elsie Clews. "A Few Zuni Death Beliefs and Practices." *American Anthropologist*, Vol. 18, Issue 2. October 28, 2009, p. 250.
7. Morell, Virginia. "The Zuni Way." *The Smithsonian*, April 2007.
8. Ibid.
9. Coburn, Kelly M., Edward Landa, Gail Wagner. "Of Silt and Ancient Voices: Water and the Zuni Land and People." National Center for Case Study Teaching in Science.
10. Morell.
11. Bonvillain, Nancy. *The Zuni* (New York: Chelsea House, 2011), pp. 33–36.

Chapter 5

1. Weiderman, Paul. "Hearts Beating in the Rock: The Zuni Show." *Santa Fe New Mexican*. August 19, 2016.
2. "Zuni Tribe of the Zuni Reservation." AAANativeArts.com
3. Ibid.
4. "Discover the Pueblo of Zuni: The Tradition and the Art of Halona Idiwan'a." Zuni Pueblo Department of Tourism.
5. Woodard, Stephanie. "Zuni Sanctuary for Injured Eagles Bestows Blessings on Birds and Caregivers." *Indian Country Today*. October 15, 2012.
6. "52nd Annual Zuni Tribal Fair Poster."
7. "Zuni Tribe of the Zuni Reservation."

Works Consulted

"52nd Annual Zuni Tribal Fair Poster." http://www.ashiwi.org/News/2016%20Fair%20Poster.pdf

"AD 1540: The Zuni Resist a Conquistador but Retreat from Spanish Guns." *Native Voices*. U.S. National Library of Medicine. Native Peoples' Concept of Health and Illness. https://www.nlm.nih.gov/nativevoices/timeline/188.html

Bond, Ann. "Zuni Crew Preserves Ancestors' Legacy." *The Cortez Journal*, October 26, 2016. http://www.cortezjournal.com/article/20161025/NEWS01/161029900/-1news&source=RSS

Bonvillain, Nancy. *The Zuni*. New York: Chelsea House, 2011.

Coburn, Kelly M., Edward Landa, Gail Wagner. "Of Silt and Ancient Voices: Water and the Zuni Land and People." National Center for Case Study Teaching in Science. http://sciencecases.lib.buffalo.edu/cs/files/zuni.pdf

"Discover the Pueblo of Zuni: The Tradition and the Art of Halona Idiwan'a." Zuni Pueblo Department of Tourism. http://www.zunitourism.com/

Drye, Willie. "Seven Cities of Cibola Legend Lures Conquistadors." *National Geographic*, n.d. http://science.nationalgeographic.com/science/archaeology/seven-cities-of-cibola/

"History of American Indian Jewelry Making." *American Indian Originals*. http://americanindianoriginals.com/jewelry-making2.html

ICTMN Staff, "Zunis Perform Ceremonial Dance for the Winter Solstice." *Indian Country Today*, December 21, 2011. http://indiancountrytodaymedianetwork.com/2011/12/21/zunis-perform-ceremonial-dance-winter-solstice-68802

McFeely, Eliza. *Zuni and the American Imagination*. New York: Hill and Wang, 2001.

Morell, Virginia. "The Zuni Way." *The Smithsonian*, April 2007. http://www.smithsonianmag.com/people-places/the-zuni-way-150866547/

"Native American Legends: The Zuni: A Mysterious People." *Legends of America*. http://www.legendsofamerica.com/na-zuni.html

Ostler, James, Marian Rodee, and Milford Nahohai. *Zuni: A Village of Silversmiths*. Santa Fe: Zuni A'Shiwi Publishing and the University of New Mexico, 1996.

Padgett, Ken. "Guide to Hopi Kachina Dolls." Kachina.us, 2005. http://kachina.us/

Parsons, Elsie Clews. "A Few Zuni Death Beliefs and Practices." *American Anthropologist*, Vol. 18, Issue 2, October 28, 2009. http://onlinelibrary.wiley.com/doi/10.1525/aa.1916.18.2.02a00060/pdf

"Prayer Sticks." *War Paths to Peace Pipes*. http://www.warpaths2peacepipes.com/native-american-culture/prayer-stick.htm

Romero, Christine. "Arizona Man Helps Preserve Zuni Language." *Deseret News*, August 27, 2006. http://www.deseretnews.com/article/645196528/Arizona-man-helps-preserve-Zuni-language.html?pg=all

"Soyal Solstice Ceremony." *War Paths to Peace Pipes.* http://www.warpaths2peacepipes.com/native-american-culture/soyal-solstice-ceremony.htm

Weiderman, Paul. "Hearts Beating in the Rock: The Zuni Show." *Santa Fe New Mexican*, August 19, 2016. http://www.santafenewmexican.com/pasatiempo/art/hearts-beating-in-the-rock-the-zuni-show/article_26a740ee-2927-5a66-b6db-788b618210e4.html

"We-Wha." PBS.org. http://www.pbs.org/outofthepast/past/p2/1886.html

Widner, Ellis. "Fetish Carvers Show How It's Done." *Philly.com*, March 4,1994. http://articles.philly.com/1994-03-04/news/25849073_1_fetishes-zuni-tradition-marian-rodee

Woodard, Stephanie. "Zuni Sanctuary for Injured Eagles Bestows Blessings on Birds and Caregivers." *Indian Country Today*, October 15, 2012. http://indiancountrytodaymedianetwork.com/2012/10/15/zuni-sanctuary-injured-eagles-bestows-blessings-birds-and-caregivers-139908

"Zuni." *World History*, September 4, 2015. http://www.worldhistory.biz/modern-history/81707-zuni.html

"Zuni—Economy." *Countries and Their Cultures.* http://www.
everyculture.com/North-America/Zuni-Economy.html

"Zuni Tribe." *War Paths to Peace Pipes.* http://www.
warpaths2peacepipes.com/indian-tribes/zuni-tribe.htm

"Zuni Tribe of the Zuni Reservation." AAANativeArts.com https://www.
aaanativearts.com/us-tribes-w-to-z/zuni-tribe-of-the-zuni-reservation

Books

Buellis, Linda. *Pueblo* (Spotlight on Native Americans). New York:
PowerKids Press, 2016.

Cunningham, Kevin, and Peter Benoit. *The Zuni.* New York: Children's
Press, 2011.

Day, Jonathan Warm. *Taos Pueblo* (Painted Stories). Santa Fe: Clear
Light Publishers, 2010.

Dressman, John. *On the Cliffs of Acoma: A Pueblo Story with a Short
History of Acoma.* Santa Fe: Sunstone Press, 2016.

Manning, Jack. *Pueblos* (American Indian Homes). North Mankato,
MN: Capstone, 2014.

On the Internet

History for Kids: Pueblo Tribe
http://www.historyforkids.net/pueblo-tribe.html

Native American History Facts: "Zuni Indian Tribe Facts"
http://native-american-indian-facts.com/Southwest-American-Indian-
Facts/Zuni-Indian-Tribe-Facts.shtml

aggressive (uh-GREH-siv)—Determined to fight.

ambassador (am-BAS-uh-der)—A person who represents a government or group.

ancestor (AN-ses-ter)—Any person in someone's family from the past.

berdache (ber-DASH)—A person of one gender who lives as another.

breechcloth (BREECH-cloth)—A cloth worn around the waist that covers front and back.

chongo (CHONG-oh)—A hairstyle in which long hair is twisted into a figure eight.

fetish (FEH-tish)—A carved figure made out of stone.

friar (FRY-ur)—A member of a religious order.

initiation (ih-nih-shee-AY-shun)—A list of tasks a person has to do in order to join a group.

irrigation (eer-ih-GAY-shun)—Moving water from a natural source to fields planted in dry areas.

kachina (ka-CHI-na)—The divine spirits of ancestors who serve as intermediaries between gods and people.

kiva (KEE-vah)—A sacred room built underground.

linguist (LING-wist)—A person who studies languages.

mesa (MAY-suh)—A flat-topped hill with steep walls.

mourn (MORN)—To express sadness over a death or loss.

nomad (NOH-mad)—A member of a group that keeps moving for survival reasons.

paternal (puh-TER-nul)—From the father's side of the family.

pueblo (PWAY-bloh)—A home or village of Native American homes built from adobe.

radius (RAY-dee-us)—The distance from the center of a circle to its edge.

silversmith (SIL-ver-smith)—A person who makes things out of silver.

solstice (SOL-stis)—Either the longest or the shortest day of the year.

MEET THE
AUTHOR

Tamra Orr is the author of more than 450 nonfiction books for readers of all ages. She lives in the Pacific Northwest with her husband and children. She graduated from Ball State University and has been writing ever since. When Orr is not researching and writing a book, she is writing letters, reading books, and camping in the incredibly beautiful state of Oregon.